AF228556

TESLA

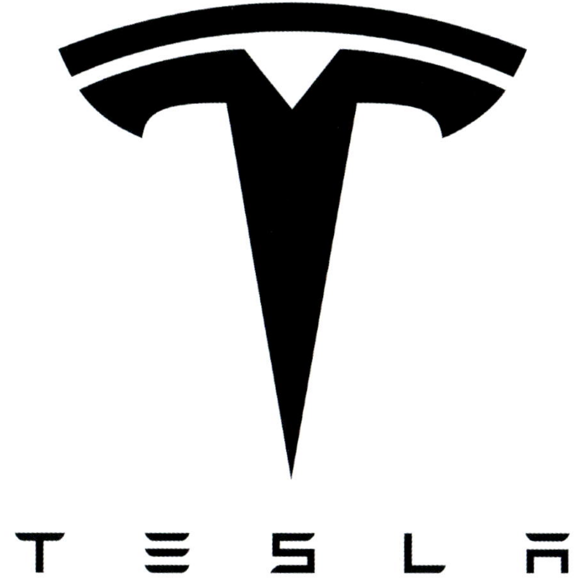

An imprint of Abdo Publishing
abdobooks.com

S.L. HAMILTON

ABDOBOOKS.COM

Published by Abdo Publishing, a division of ABDO, PO Box 398166, Minneapolis, Minnesota 55439. Copyright © 2023 by Abdo Consulting Group, Inc. International copyrights reserved in all countries. No part of this book may be reproduced in any form without written permission from the publisher. A&D Xtreme™ is a trademark and logo of Abdo Publishing.

Printed in China

052022
092022

Editor: John Hamilton

Copy Editor: Tamara L. Britton

Graphic Design: Sue Hamilton

Cover Design: Laura Graphenteen

Cover Photo: Shutterstock

Interior Photos & Illustrations: All images Tesla, Inc., except: Alamy-pgs 32-33; Astrum People-pg 6 (inset); Car and Bike-pg 7 (inset); Shutterstock-pgs 4-5, 21 (top), 24-25 & 36-37; US Navy-pg 40 (inset).

LIBRARY OF CONGRESS CONTROL NUMBER: 2021942760

PUBLISHER'S CATALOGING-IN-PUBLICATION DATA

Names: Hamilton, S.L., author.

Title: Tesla / by S.L. Hamilton

Description: Minneapolis, Minnesota : Abdo Publishing, 2023 | Series: Xtreme cars | Includes online resources and index.

Identifiers: ISBN 9781532196102 (lib. bdg.) | ISBN 9781098217037 (ebook)

Subjects: LCSH: Tesla automobiles--Juvenile literature. | Sports cars--Juvenile literature. | Cars (Automobiles)--Juvenile literature.

Classification: DDC 629.2221--dc23

TABLE OF **CONTENTS**

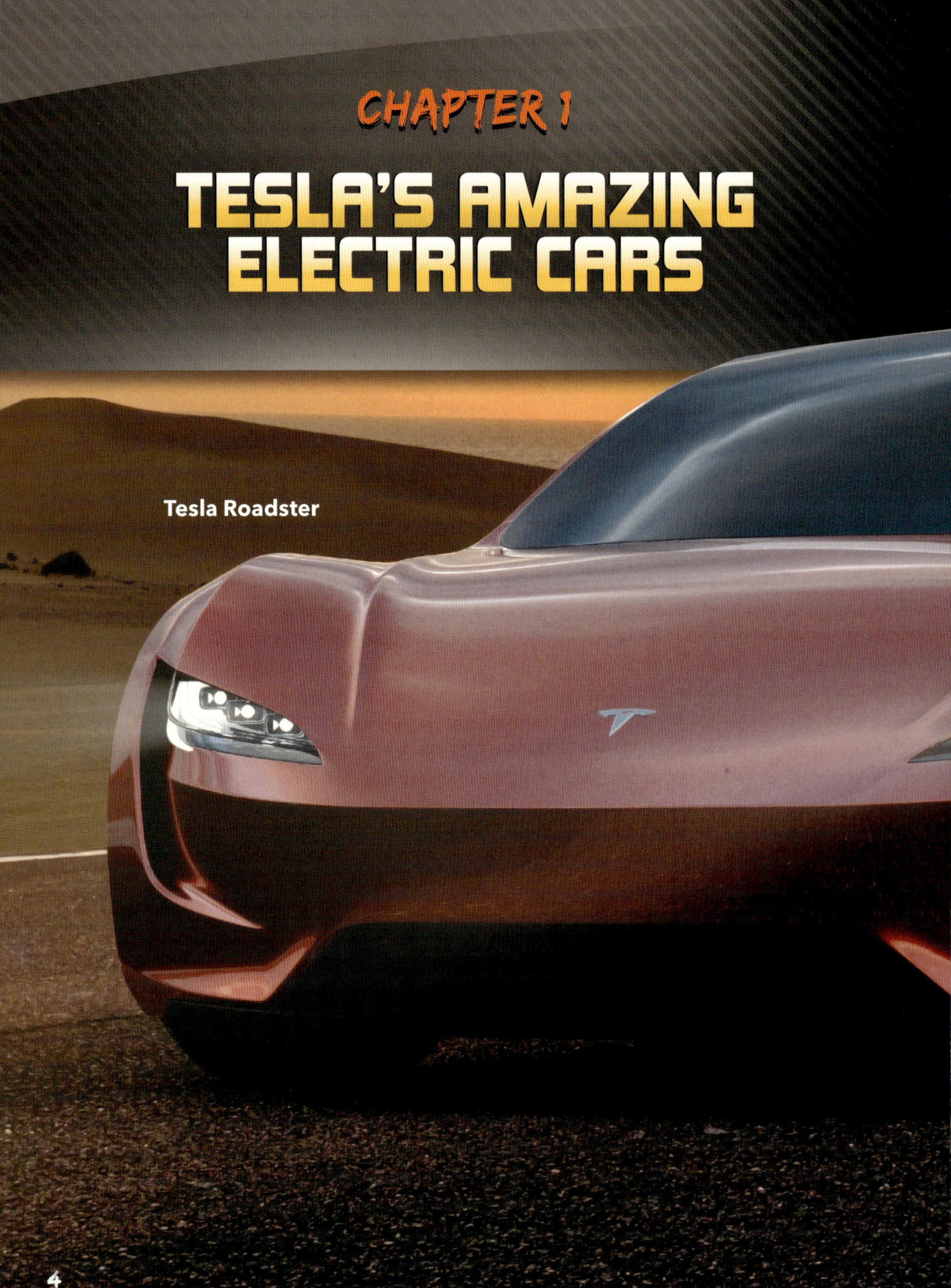

CHAPTER 1
TESLA'S AMAZING
ELECTRIC CARS
Tesla Roadster

Tesla's **eco-friendly** vehicles have electrified the automobile market since 2008. The plug-in electric cars are fast and futuristic looking.

XTREME FACT

Tesla was named after Nikola Tesla (1856-1943), an award-winning engineer and inventor known for his work with electric power.

CHAPTER 2

HISTORY: STARTING TESLA MOTORS

Tesla Motors was started in 2003 by Marc Tarpenning and Martin Eberhard, with a majority of funding money from Elon Musk. Their plan was to develop an American electric sports car that could cleanly perform with the same power as gasoline-powered sports cars.

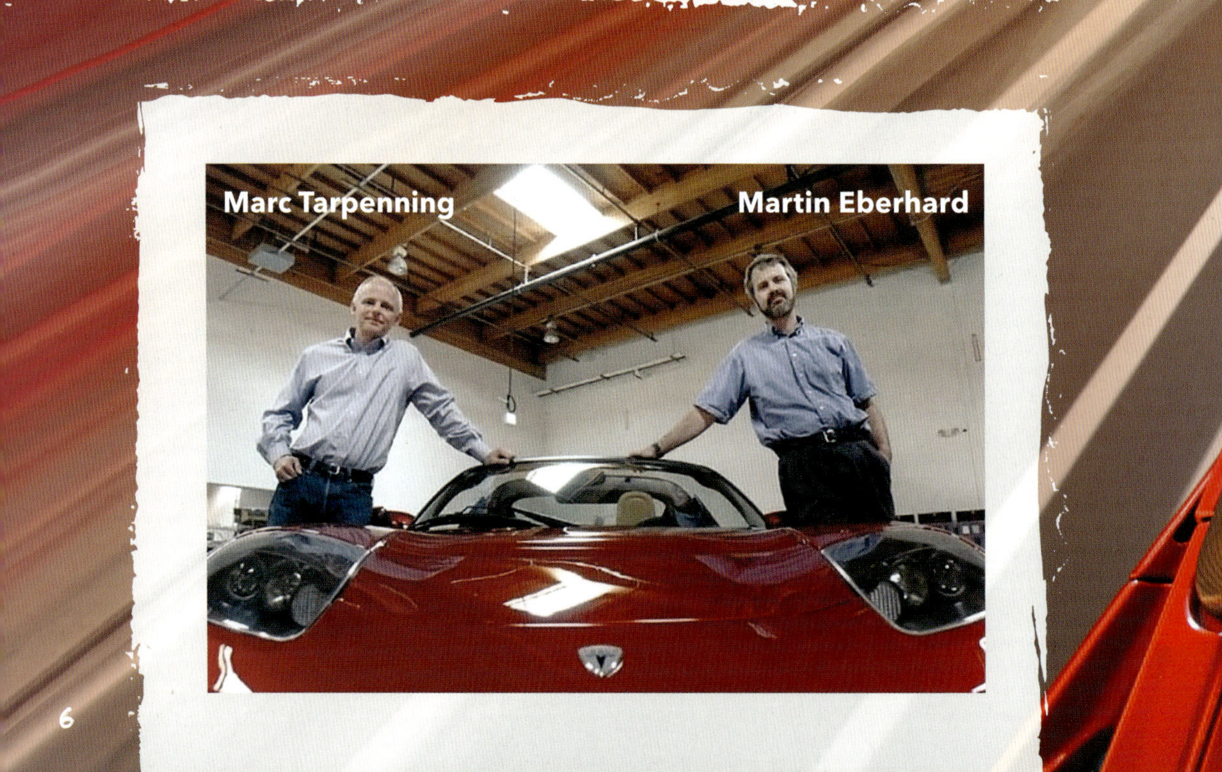

Elon Musk began heading up the company in 2008, the same year the Tesla Roadster was released. It was powered by **lithium-ion cells** and could be recharged from a standard electric outlet.

Elon Musk

CHAPTER 3

FIRST GENERATION ROADSTER

The all-electric first generation Tesla Roadster went an amazing 245 miles (394 km) on a single charge. Its top speed was 125 mph (201 kph). The 2-seater was expensive, ranging in cost from $80,000-$120,000.

ROADSTER SPECIFICATIONS

YEARS PRODUCED
2008-2012

MAXIMUM HORSEPOWER
288 (model 2.5)

ZERO TO 60 MPH (97 KPH)
4 seconds

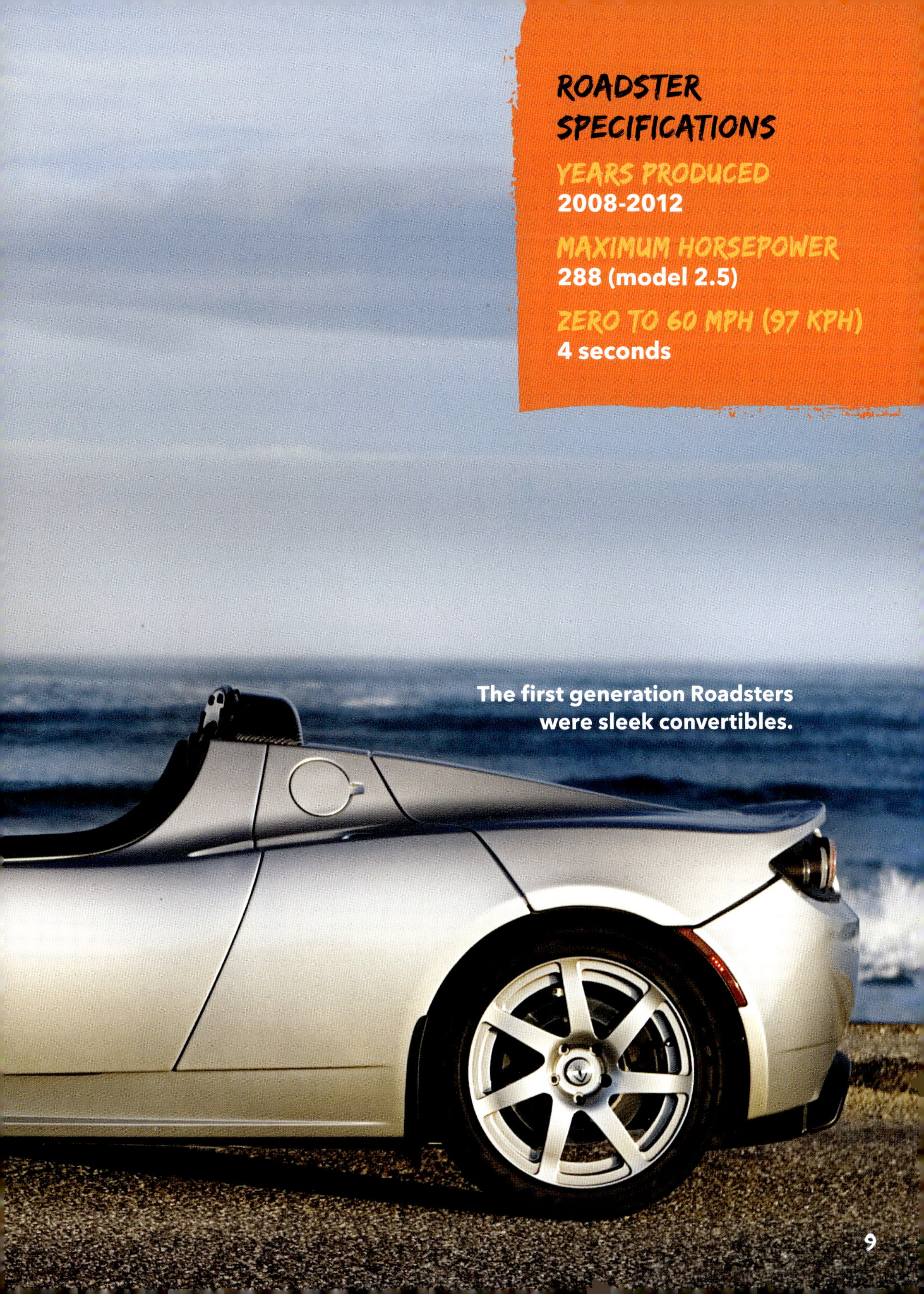

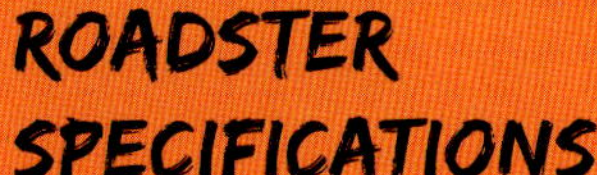

The first generation Roadsters were sleek convertibles.

The Roadster's lightweight body was made of **carbon fiber**. The lower weight helped it get amazing mileage. It equaled a gas-powered car getting 135 miles per gallon (57 kpl), but without noise or polluting **emissions**.

Only 2,500 models of the Roadster two-seat electric sports car were built.

XTREME FACT

Elon Musk also owns SpaceX. Musk's first generation Roadster was shot into space as payload on a SpaceX test flight on February 6, 2018.

CHAPTER 4

MODEL S ELECTRIC SEDAN

Tesla's Model S came out in 2012. This electric **sedan** could travel 265 miles (426 km) on a single charge. The battery recharged 3 times faster than most plug-in cars. Its top speed was 130 mph (209 kph).

XTREME FACT

Beginning in 2014, Model S cars included an autopilot feature. Drivers needed to supervise, but a self-driving electric car had arrived.

The Model S won Motor Trend's
Car of the Year award in 2012.

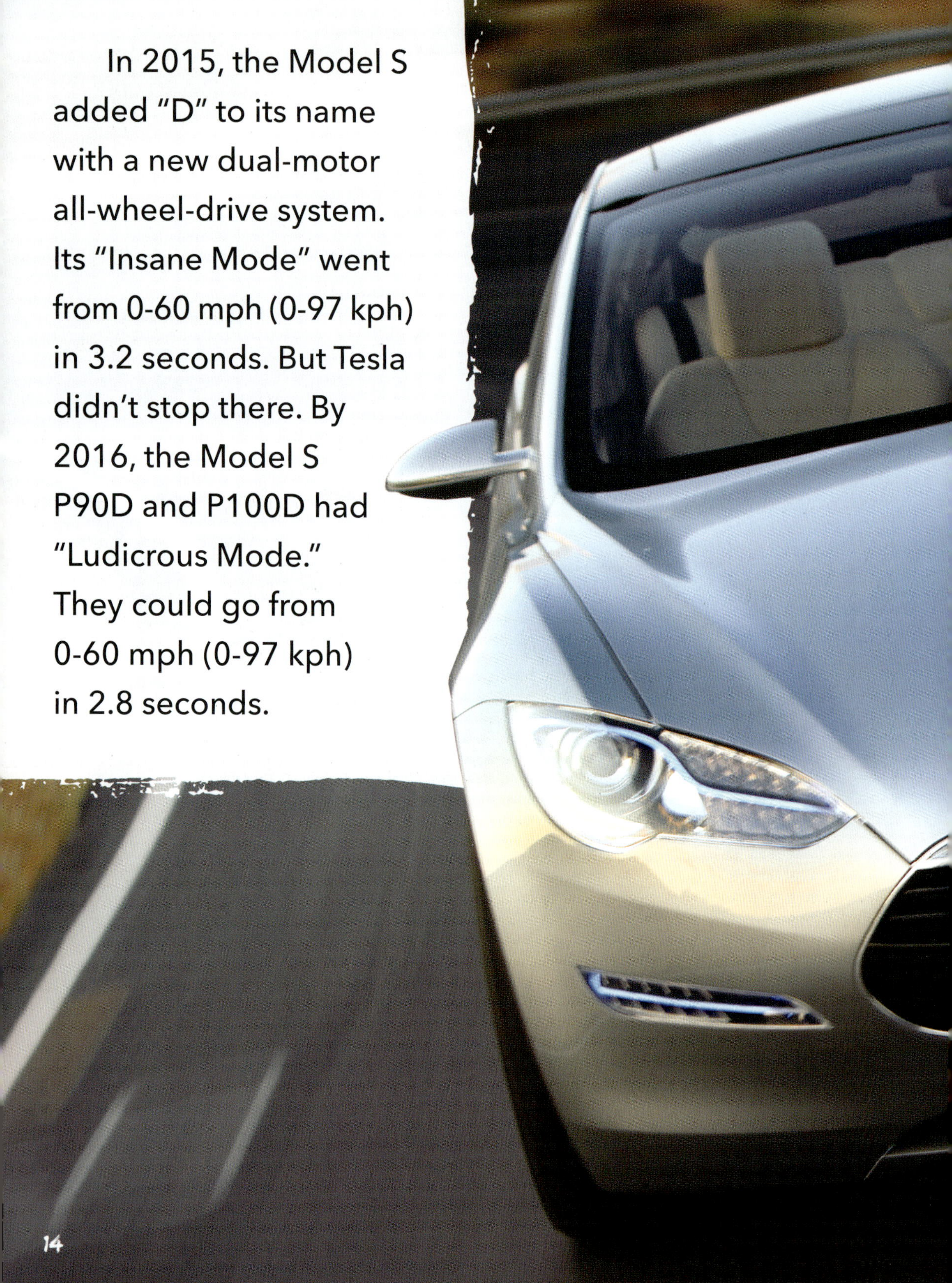

In 2015, the Model S added "D" to its name with a new dual-motor all-wheel-drive system. Its "Insane Mode" went from 0-60 mph (0-97 kph) in 3.2 seconds. But Tesla didn't stop there. By 2016, the Model S P90D and P100D had "Ludicrous Mode." They could go from 0-60 mph (0-97 kph) in 2.8 seconds.

The Model S's all-wheel drive system gave the car added traction on the road for better performance.

The 2021 Model S Plaid has the longest range and quickest acceleration of any electric **production car**. It can go 390 miles (628 km) and reach 60 mph/97 kph in 1.99 seconds. Its top speed is 200 mph (322 kph).

Drivers can use the Model S's touch screen for information on their car and route. They can even play video games when they aren't driving.

The interior features a 17" central display screen. Turn signals, lights, and horn are touch buttons on the yoke-like steering wheel. There is no gear shift because the Plaid's computer senses which direction the driver wants to go.

CHAPTER 5

CHARGER STATIONS

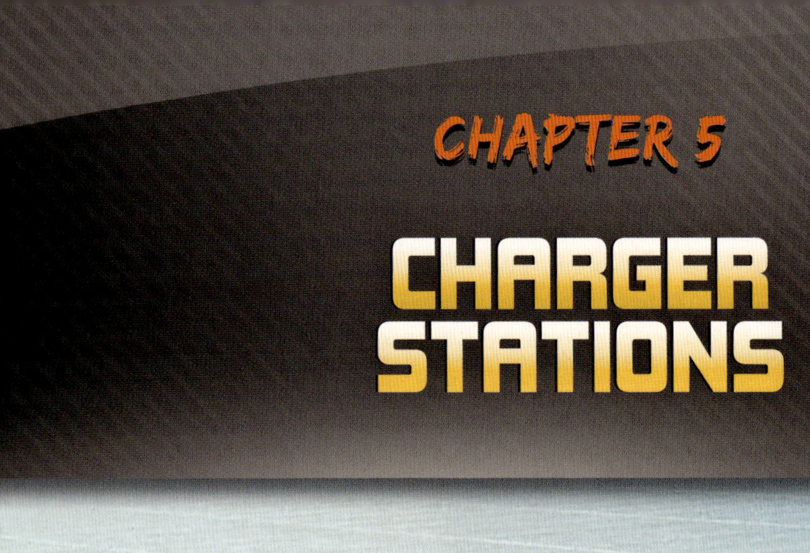

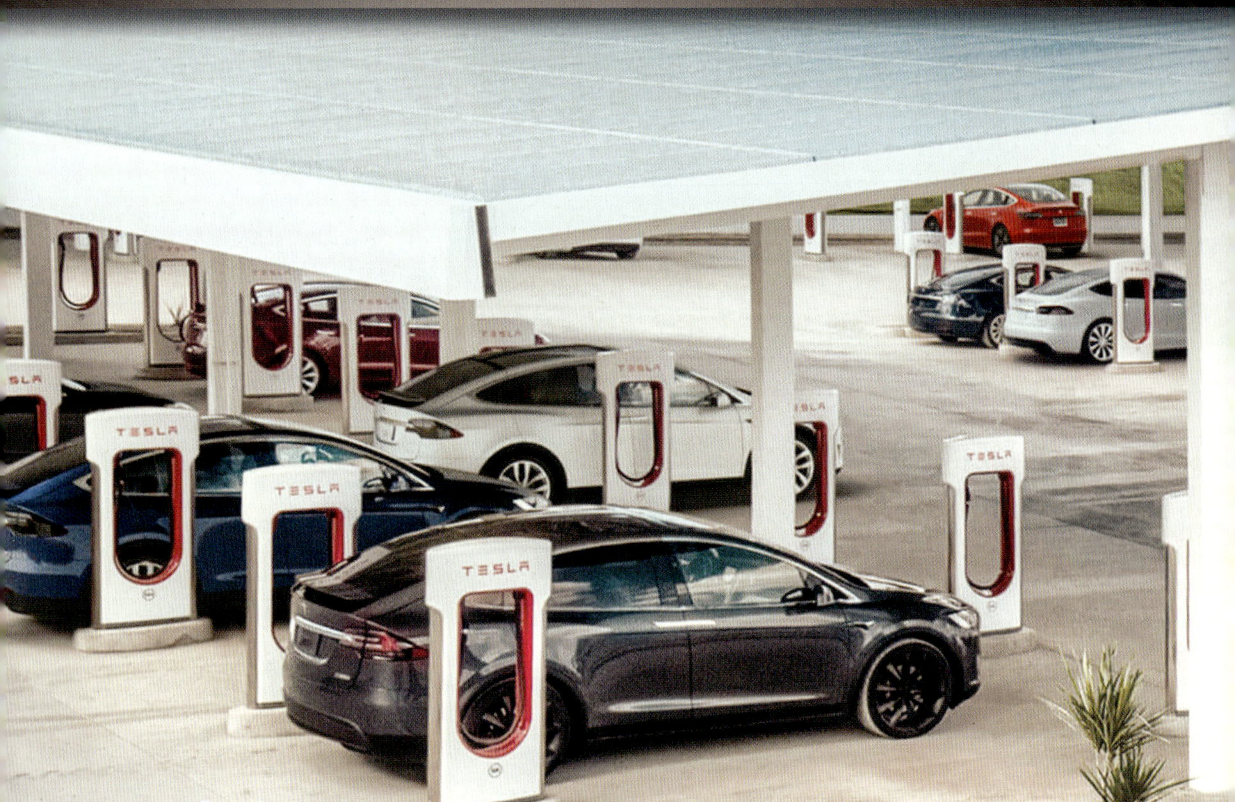

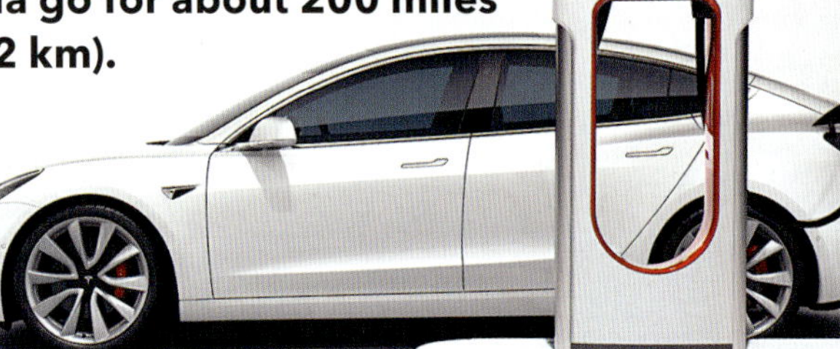

A 15-minute charge lets a Tesla go for about 200 miles (322 km).

For Teslas to go cross country, Supercharger stations began to be setup in 2012. These fast-charging sites are like traditional gas stations. They allow owners to plug in, charge, and go in 15 minutes. Some owners even receive free charging for certain Tesla models.

Tesla also has "destination chargers." These are set up at popular places such as hotels, restaurants, and stores. However, they do not recharge the vehicle as fast as Supercharger sites. A Tesla app lets owners know where to find the nearest charger station.

A phone app lets owners see their Tesla's battery charge.

Older model Teslas had the charger port on the side of the car. Newer Teslas have the port hidden behind the car's taillight.

CHAPTER 6

MODEL X ELECTRIC SUV

In 2017, Tesla introduced the Model X sport utility vehicle (SUV). It features the most storage space and towing capacity of any electric SUV. A Model X can go as far as 360 miles (579 km) on a single charge.

The Model X seats up to 7 people. It goes farther on a single charge than any other electric SUV.

Model X's rear falcon-wing doors are also known as gull-wing doors or up-doors.

The Model X's features include front doors that open and close automatically. Its back falcon-wing doors are hinged on the roof. This makes it easier to load and unload. The Model X's **aerodynamic** styling helps give it a top speed of 163 mph (262 kph).

CHAPTER 7

MODEL 3 SEDAN

In 2017, Tesla introduced the ultra-safe Model 3 **sedan**. It features an aluminum and steel frame. Even with its all-glass roof, it can withstand four times its own mass in crush tests. With a top speed of 162 mph (261 kph), it travels 353 miles (568 km) on a charge.

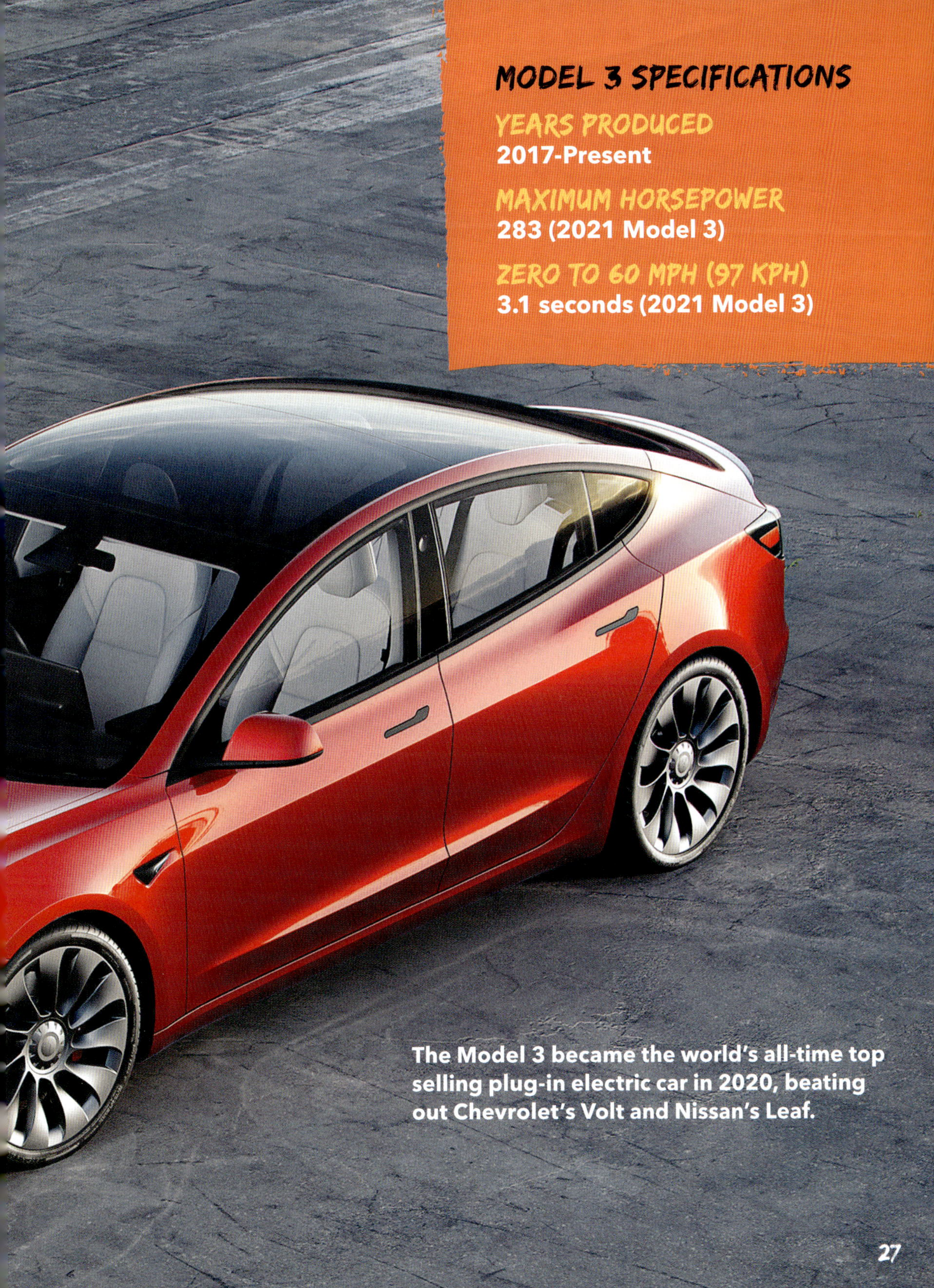

The Model 3 became the world's all-time top selling plug-in electric car in 2020, beating out Chevrolet's Volt and Nissan's Leaf.

The Model 3 has the highest safety ratings
and lowest chance of injury of all cars.

The Model 3 has been built around the driver. Its windows plus the all-glass roof allow great visibility. The **minimalist** interior features a 15-inch (38-cm) touchscreen display that puts everything at the driver's fingertips.

XTREME FACT

In a safety crush test, the Model 3's glass roof was able to withstand the same weight as two full-grown African elephants.

TESLA GIGAFACTORIES

Giga Shanghai began being built in 2018. Only a year later, their first Model 3s rolled off the assembly line.

XTREME FACT

When fully completed, Tesla expects its Gigafactories to be the biggest buildings in the world. Each one will be powered by renewable energy, such as solar or wind.

Tesla opened its first factory in Fremont, California, in 2010. However, to keep up with demand for its best-selling, plug-in vehicles, Tesla went on to build huge manufacturing plants. Each is known as Gigafactory. Giga Nevada opened in 2016. Others quickly followed, including Giga New York, Giga Shanghai (China), Giga Berlin (Germany), and Giga Texas.

Tesla employs from 2,000-7,000 people in each Gigafactory. Different factories produce different parts and vehicles. For example, Giga Nevada makes

lithium-ion cells and other electric vehicle parts. Giga Shanghai does the final assembly of many Model 3s and Model Ys. They plan to produce up to 500,000 cars a year.

Tesla's Giga Shanghai
manufacturing plant

CHAPTER 9

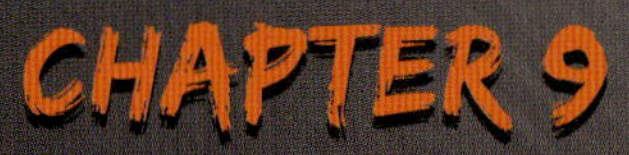

MODEL Y COMPACT SUV

The Model Y is an electric, all-wheel-drive, compact SUV. Its dual motor system includes a powerful rear motor that helps its off-roading abilities. The Model Y can travel for 326 miles (525 km) on a charge, with a top speed of 135 mph (217 kph).

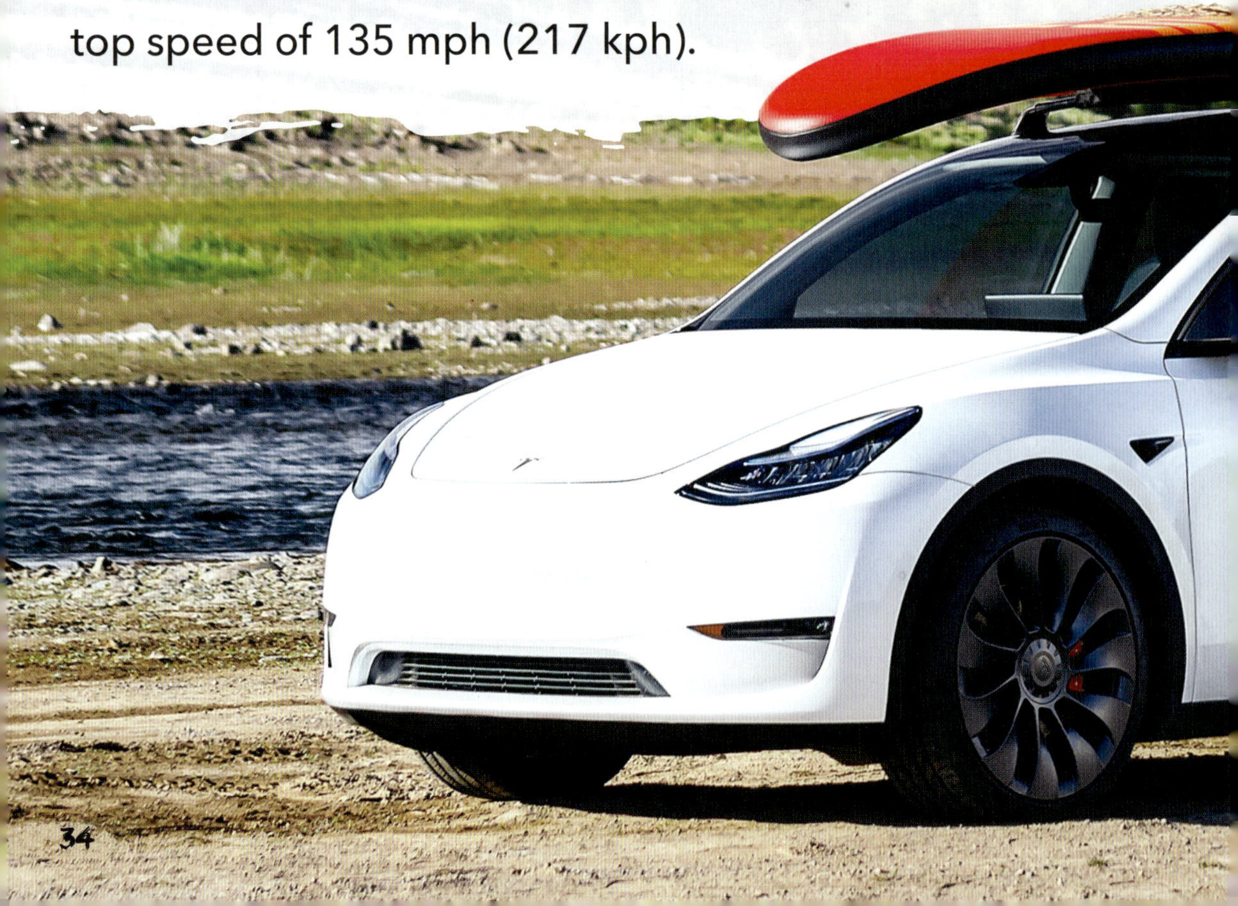

MODEL Y SPECIFICATIONS
YEARS PRODUCED
2017-Present
MAXIMUM HORSEPOWER
384 (2021 Long Range)
ZERO TO 60 MPH (97 KPH)
3.5 seconds (2021 Long Range)

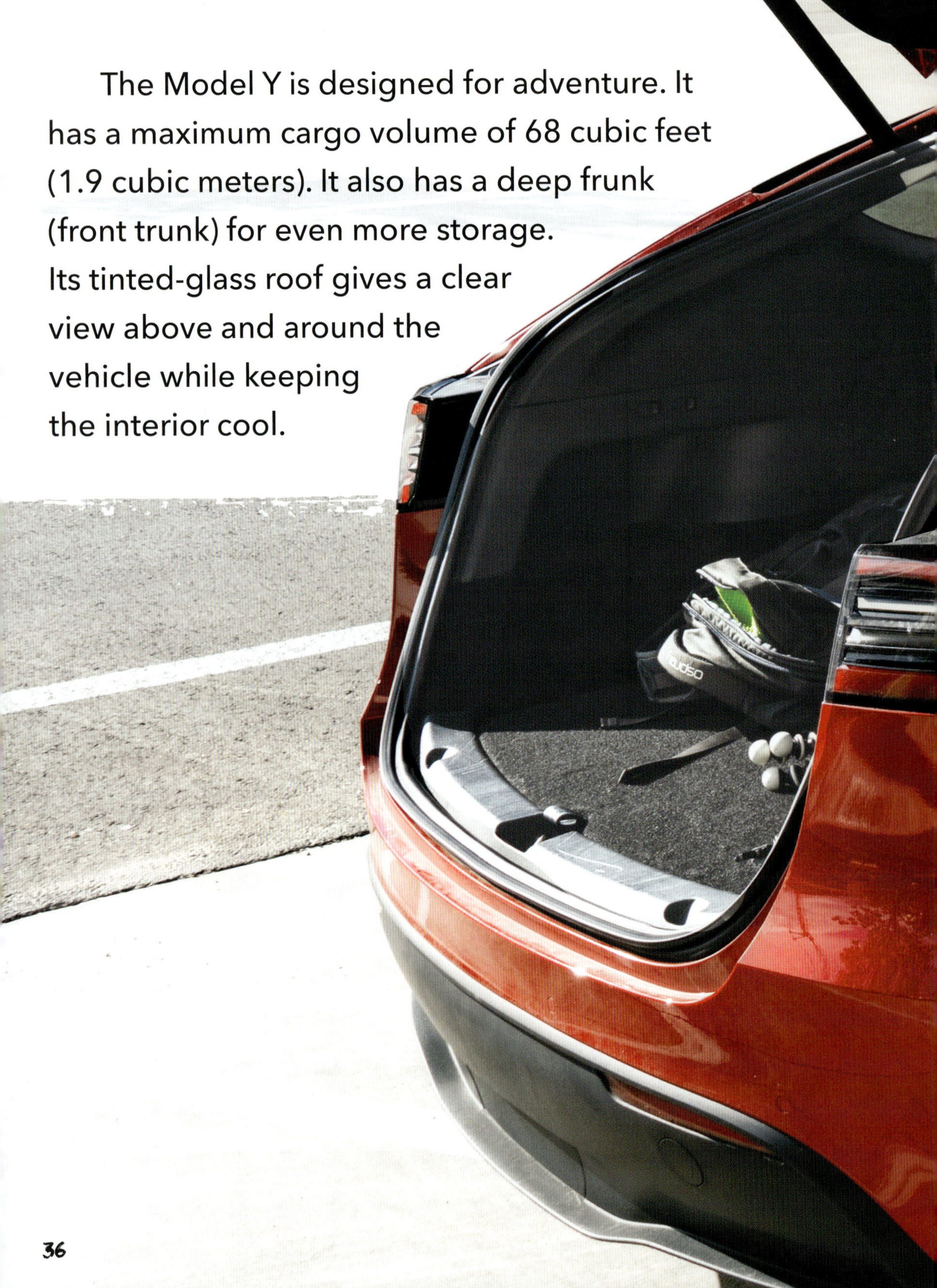

The Model Y is designed for adventure. It has a maximum cargo volume of 68 cubic feet (1.9 cubic meters). It also has a deep frunk (front trunk) for even more storage. Its tinted-glass roof gives a clear view above and around the vehicle while keeping the interior cool.

Model Y
Frunk

TESLA'S CYBERTRUCK

The Cybertruck has the high performance of a sports car with the power of a pickup truck. Its stainless-steel and armored glass design is futuristic and tough. It has a top speed of 110 mph (177 kph) and can go up to 500 miles (805 km) on a single charge.

Tesla calls the Cybertruck's stainless-steel skin an "exoskeleton." It does not rust and easily withstands dents and damage.

The Cybertruck holds 100 cubic feet (2.8 cubic meters) of storage and up to 3,500 pounds (1,588 kg) of **payload**. It has a built-in ramp for loading. The Cybertruck self-balances itself with heavy payloads. It can tow up to 14,000 pounds (6,350 kg).

XTREME FACT

The US Navy's new USS *Zumwalt* destroyer was one of the inspirations for the Cybertruck's unique design.

The Cybertruck is so tough, its steel body is bulletproof.

Lockable Bed Cover

The Vault

Secret Storage

Built-In Ramp

The Cybertruck has several automatic systems. Some models are fully self driving and have automatic parking and trailer docking. The Cybertruck's 17-inch (43-cm) touchscreen computer provides complete information

to the driver. Similar to the Model S, the Cybertruck has a race car-like steering yoke. The dashboard looks like marble, but is actually made of an environmentally friendly paper and **resin** blend.

CHAPTER 11

THE FUTURE

Tesla's future electric vehicles will go farther and faster. The company plans to release a second generation Roadster with new upgrades and styling. With an estimated 0-60 mph (0-97 kph) in 1.9 seconds, it may become the fastest **production car** in the world.

Tesla's future Roadster will be a convertible.

XTREME CHALLENGE

1) Who started Tesla Motors?

2) What was the first electric car that Tesla produced?

3) What type of battery is used to power a Tesla vehicle?

4) Which model of car was Telsa's first sedan? What speed modes did it have?

5) How many minutes does it take to charge a Tesla at a Supercharger station?

6) The Model X SUV has what type of unique rear doors?

7) What is the name of the Tesla's huge manufacturing sites?

8) What Tesla vehicle is made of stainless steel and armored glass?

GLOSSARY

aerodynamic – Something that has a shape that reduces the drag, or resistance, of air moving across its surface. Sports cars with aerodynamic shapes can go faster because they don't have to push as hard to get through the air.

carbon fiber – A very strong, thin, and lightweight fiber made of carbon atoms. It may be used in the bodies of cars, planes, and boats.

eco-friendly – Something that does not pollute the environment.

emissions – Engines that are powered by burning fossil fuels, such as gasoline, produce pollutants. These cause environmental concerns because of their effect on air quality. Electric vehicles have no polluting emissions.

lithium-ion cells – Units that make up lithium-ion batteries. These lightweight, rechargeable batteries use a lithium-ion solution to provide stored power.

minimalist – A simple, clean design without added decorations.

payload – The maximum amount of weight a vehicle can safely carry in the cargo area or truck bed.

production car – A model of car that is produced by a company that all look the same and are sold to the public.

resin – A thick, fairly clear liquid substance that is often made from tree sap. Artificial resins have also been produced in labs. Resin may be combined with other substances to create a hard, naturally protective product.

sedan – An automobile with a hard, permanent roof that has two or four doors and seats four or more people. It is sometimes considered to be a family car.

ONLINE RESOURCES

To learn more about Tesla, please visit abdobooklinks.com or scan this QR code. These links are routinely monitored and updated to provide the most current information available.

INDEX